Inside Stories

Book 2

DL 401

Written by **Janice Montgomery** and **Candace Taff Carr**   Illustrated by **Jean Thornley**

Edited by Dianne Draze and Sandy Woolley

The following units were written by Sandy Woolley:
Dear Mr. Henshaw and The Lion, The Witch and the Wardrobe.

ISBN 0-931724-50-3

Contents

For the Instructor

Why Teach Literature?

The ability to communicate distinguishes humans from other forms of animal life. This ability to communicate has enabled us to not only meet our most basic needs but also to share our most eloquent thoughts and lofty dreams. When these thoughts and impressions are shared in the form of written language, they become literature. For the reader, literature is one form of self-expression that can take us beyond the limitations of our own situation and carry us to other times and places. Without moving from our comfortable chair, we can experience distant places and travel into the past and future. Without risking bodily injury, we can vicariously take part in breath-taking adventures. We can try on different personalities, experiment with new ideas, and feel a wide range of emotions. Through the pages of a book, we can take part in a life far grander and more diversified than the one we actually live.

Literature should be an integral part of the reading program for all students. Literature gives students an opportunity to apply the skills that are developed through basal readers and workbooks. It entertains while building the ability to imagine and developing intellectual skills. It gives readers the opportunity to think about feelings, morals, and values and helps them define the relationships between other people. Literature exploration takes students beyond skill building and lets them grown intellectually, emotionally, and in aesthetic appreciation.

Helping children appreciate literature and instilling a love of reading is perhaps one of the most precious gifts a teacher can give his or her students. We are glad that you chose *Inside Stories* to help you with this task. We are sure that these guides will provide many hours of reading enjoyment and material for thought provoking.

About This Book

This book is one in a series entitled *Inside Stories*. Each book contains ten literature guides. The books have been grouped according to grade levels and include a variety of literature types. Each edition is designed to introduce students to several different genres of literature as well as a variety of skills. These texts were developed in the Bartholomew Consolidated School Corporation for use with fourth through eighth grade students. The intent is to give teachers an easyto-use vehicle to introduce students to literature appreciation and analysis.

These study guides were designed to be used in a situation in which the teacher directs discussion groups consisting of a small group of students. They can also be used with cluster grouping or with an entire class with aides or volunteers serving as discussion leaders.

Each book in this series consists of the following materials:

1. Instructors' Notes

This page includes suggested grade levels, a brief biography of the author, a synopsis of the book, suggestions for themes, literary objectives (including exploration of the plot, character development, themes, and writing techniques), and a list of companion titles. Instructors will find this page helpful in planning the general direction and specific goals they wish to accomplish for a book.

2. Reading Assignments

These reproducible pages break the novel into manageable sections and provide vocabulary words and questions for each reading assignment. For some books, the list of vocabulary words is quite extensive, so instructors may wish to select only some of the suggested vocabulary words. Questions are designed to test students' comprehension of the material but also to draw them into higher-level thinking. Instructors may ask students to write the answers to the questions before discussing them as a group. These questions are not the single-answer or fill-in-the-blank variety. Therefore, students should be encouraged to provide complete, thoughtful answers. An answer page or section with specific answers is not given, because this would tend to indicate that there is one "right" answer. Instead, as answers are discussed, instructors should ask for explanations and justifications rather than settling for a single correct answer. Many of the questions ask for interpretations or evaluations. It can be expected, therefore, that students will have a variety of answers and should be given the opportunity to discuss and compare their ideas.

3. Conclusion and Summary

This reproducible page looks at the entire book and draws all elements into focus. These questions require higher-level thinking skills of analysis, synthesis, and evaluation and divergent interpretations. They are intended to give students an opportunity to draw comparisons and conclusions and to apply ideas to their own lives. Students should be asked to review each question carefully and give answers that reflect their understanding of the entire story. They should use examples and quotations to support their answers wherever appropriate.

4. Activities

This reproducible page presents several enrichment activities to expand students' understanding of the book. These activities are a combination of research or individual interpretation of the concepts presented in the book and a finished product that is the vehicle for displaying or communicating those ideas. Students should be instructed to select those activities that enable them to use their creative abilities and present their ideas about the book. Instructors may wish to work with individual students to create other activities that will be showcases for their ideas about the book or provide opportunities for doing in-depth research on individually-selected topics.

Behavioral Objectives

As a result of using the materials in this book, students may be expected to accomplish the following:

1. Students will develop an awareness and appreciation of a wide variety of good literature.
2. Students will develop and make use of the higher-level thinking skills of analysis, synthesis, and evaluation.
3. Students will develop oral and written communication skills.
4. Students will increase their written and oral vocabulary.
5. Students will understand and be able to recognize the elements of a story (setting, problem, climax, and ending).
6. Students will understand, be able to recognize, and be able to create their own samples of literary techniques and strategies.
7. Students will be able to identify themes and apply concepts presented in the books to their own lives.
8. Students will be able to make judgments concerning morals and values as presented in the books.
9. Students will be able to analyze characters, their traits, motives, and feelings and compare characters to themselves.

Instructor's Role

The instructor plays an important role in bringing literary works to life in the classroom. It is important that students sense that the teacher values reading and literature. The literature exploration that begins in the classroom setting should spill over into all areas of students' lives. To do this, teachers need to help students discover the relationship between the situations and concepts presented in each book and their own lives. It is important, therefore, that the teacher establish an atmosphere where students feel free to express their opinions. Students should be encouraged to elaborate on their answers, justify their evaluations, and interject their own feelings. In addition to the questions that are provided, teachers should ask probing questions that will guide students to define their thoughts and feelings. There should also be less emphasis on objectives testing and more emphasis on subjective forms of evaluation. This would include evaluating students' learning via written assignments, essays, reports, activities, and discussions.

Ben And Me
Robert Lawson

Suggested Reading Level
Grades 4-5

Biography
    Robert Lawson was born in New York City on October 4, 1892. Raised in a New Jersey suburb, he later moved to Westport, Connecticut with his writer, illustrator wife and lived in a home they called Rabbit Hill. Schooled in art, Lawson was a camouflage artist in World War 1. Afterwards he became a commercial artist and then began illustrating books for adult and children's authors. The first book he wrote and illustrated himself was *Ben and Me*. He was the first man to win both of the highest awards for children's books in the U.S. In 1941, he won the Caldecott Medal for *They Were Strong and Good*, and in 1945, he won the Newbery Award for *Rabbit Hill*. Another popular historic book he wrote was *Mr. Revere and I* in 1953. Robert Lawson died May 26, 1957.

Synopsis
Historical Fiction
    This is historically accurate fiction with a twist of the unbelievable! Amos, a mouse, who lives in the domicile of statesman and inventor, Ben Franklin, tells this tale of the real story of the Revolution from the rodent's point of view, of course. Amos provides a unique and humorous view of scientist Ben, who to Amos' dismay, uses the mouse as an unwilling victim of his experiments. It is entertaining and informative.

Themes
1. Resolution of conflict between individuals and groups
2. Consideration and trust in friendships
3. Elements of greatness or fame

Literary Objectives
1. Identify and analyze the point of view
2. Contrast fiction and fantasy
3. Critique author's style and his use of humor and facts

Companion Titles
1. *Mrs. Frisby and the Rats of Nimh* – Robert C. O'Brien (use of animals to portray human qualities, resolution of conflict)
2. *Rabbit Hill* – Robert Lawson (comparison of author's style, use of animals to convey theme, resolution of conflict, consideration and trust)
3. *Johnny Tremain* – Esther Forbes (resolution of conflict, Revolutionary War period)
4. *Charlotte's Web* – E. B. White (use of animals to portray human qualities, consideration and trust in friendship)

Ben And Me

Foreword and Chapters 1–3

Vocabulary

manuscript   hoax   lamented   vestry   statesman
maxims   domicile   succor   inclement

1. How was the **authenticity** of this document proven?

2. What did Lawson, the author, infer about the differences between this account of Franklin's life and those of later historians?

3. Why was Amos writing this book?

4. How did Amos come to reside with Ben Franklin?

5. What sparked Amos' suggestion for inventing a stove?

6. What do you think "Ben was a fair terror for work" meant? What clues did you use?

7. What were the problems with a fireplace for heating a home? How did the Franklin stove improve this?

8. What was the Agreement? Was it necessary? Explain.

9. From Amos' description, what kind of person was Ben Franklin? Use carefully selected adjectives to describe Ben. Explain how you arrived at your choices.

10. Ben used maxims or proverbs. Copy one from the reading assignment and explain its meaning.

Ben And Me
Chapters 4–5

Vocabulary

barbarous   disported   ludicrous   despondency   disheveled
dissemination   idling   odious   scurrilous

1. Why did Franklin **not** heed Amos' warnings on the dangers of swimming?

2. Why did the townspeople come out to the pond? What was Ben's relationship with the public? How do you know?

3. How did Amos wreck havoc in the press room?

4. How did Ben get out of trouble?

5. When Ben said that he smelled a rat, what did he mean?

6. What was Amos' reaction when accused of the deed? Why? How might you have reacted?

7. What type of information could be found in *Poor Richard's Almanac*? Who might use this information?

Ben And Me
Chapters 6-8

Vocabulary

lenient   philosophical   prominent   disastrous   subdued
deceit   idyllic

1. Ben did not think Amos was a "person of vision." What did this mean? Give examples of people you think are or were. Tell why you chose them.

2. What do you think Ben meant when he said he hoped to "tear the lightning from the skies and harness it to do the bidding of man?"

3. What was the Philosophical Society?

4. What seemed to happen when Ben was gone and Amos was alone with Ben's equipment?

5. Why did Ben hope to prove lightning and electricity were the same thing?

6. Why did Ben refuse credit for inventing lightning rods?

7. How do you think the common folk regarded Dr. Franklin and his experiments?

8. What were the idyllic surroundings Amos enjoyed?

9. Why was Amos so hurt by Ben's deceit? Relate a personal story about a broken relationship caused by deceit.

10. Why was Ben going abroad? How might this trip help or hurt Amos and Ben's damaged friendship?

Ben And Me
Chapters 9-11

Vocabulary

foray   firebrand   eloquence   sloop   aspirations

milliner   thwart   quaint   aristocrat

1. Why were Ben and Amos' differences forgotten?

2. In what ways were Red and Thomas Jefferson like Amos and Ben?

3. What were Red's most impressive qualities?

4. What happened to Red's manifesto?

5. What were the reasons Amos especially liked George Washington?

6. What was Amos' reaction to Red's fury? With which character do you side? Why?

7. Why did the Colonies want Dr. Franklin to seek foreign aid?

8. Explain one of the maxims in Chapter 11 in relationship to Ben's task in France.

9. How did Amos intend to play "no small part in the affairs of" Sophia?

Ben And Me
Chapters 12-15

Vocabulary

trousseau   infested   uncouth   reliance   vengeance
opulent   proletariat   fickle

1. Why did Ben stay in France so long?

2. What assistance did Amos get for Sophia's plight?

3. Explain Amos' remark, "Alas for Red's faith in the proletariat."

4. When they thought they were beaten, who saved the day?

5. Why did Amos claim the French were fickle?

6. Why was Ben regarded as a hero upon his return to America?

7. Was Ben really a hero? Defend your answer.

8. Why was all well with Amos in the last chapter?

9. Why did Amos get Ben a new hat?

10. How was this book an effective approach to portraying historical fact?

Ben And Me
Conclusion and Summary

1. What, in your opinion, was Ben's greatest contribution to America? Defend your answer.

2. What makes Lawson's technique of using a mouse to tell about these events in history particulary effective? Give at least two ways.

3. Ben and Amos had a good relationship, but several factors strained their friendship. Identify the causes of these problems. How might you counsel them to overcome these problems?

4. Ben Franklin was a complex character. Choose three good adjectives that describe different aspects of his personality and give an example for each.

5. Would you define this book as historical fiction or fantasy? Defend your answer.

6. Identify three actual historical events from the book that are fictionalized by Lawson. Briefly give an accurate description of each.

7. What is creativity? Who is the most creative character in *Ben And Me*? What are the benefits of creativity?

8. Ben was hailed as a hero in America after being in France. Is being famous the same as being a hero? How are these things different? How are they the same?

9. What are some conflicts in this story? How are they resolved?

10. What if Ben Franklin were alive today? What do you think he would be doing?

Ben And Me
Activities

1. Create your own filmstrip or roller movie of *Ben And Me*. Choose twelve to twenty scenes to illustrate on 11 x 18 inch paper. Use bold, large drawings and make title and credit frames. Write a script to narrate your scenes.

2. Draw a map of Philadelphia at the time of Ben's residence there. Be sure to include details and labels.

3. Write a short story about another historic event using Lawson's technique of an animal who observes the daily routine.

4. Do an oral or written report about Benjamin Franklin or Thomas Jefferson. Include note cards and a complete bibliography.

5. Plan a school trip to Philadelphia today, including mileage, and itinerary. Give a brief description of each historic place the class should visit.

6. Make a scrapbook of Franklin's inventions, including an illustration, brief description, date, and comment on usefulness/success of the invention. Be sure to make a table of contents and a bibliography.

7. Draw an illustrated timeline of Benjamin Franklin's life from birth to death. Be sure to include all milestones, achievements, and significant events.

8. Pretend you are Ben Franklin and do a dramatic reading of his maxims. Try to sound as realistic as possible.

9. Using a shoe box, make a 3-dimensional diorama of a scene from the book.

10. Benjamin Franklin had many other adventures that Amos didn't write about. After reading about Franklin's life, choose an event and, as Amos, write a new chapter for the book.

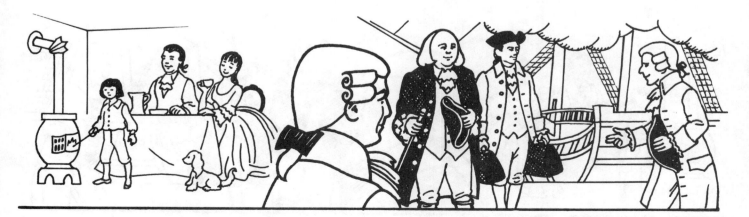

Caddie Woodlawn
Carol Ryrie Brink

Suggested Reading Level
Grade 4-5

Biography
Carol Ryrie Brink authored 27 books for children and adults before her death in 1981. Her most popular book is *Caddie Woodlawn*. Other books include *Magical Melons*, *Baby Island*, *The Pink Motel*, and *Winter Cottage*. Ms. Brink grew up listening to the stories about her grandmother's pioneer childhood in Wisconsin, which provided the basis for some of her novels. She lived in Idaho, Minnesota, and California. The mother of two, she often tried out her new books on her eight grandchildren before sending them to a publisher.

Synopsis
Caddie Woodlawn is the true story of the author's grandmother, a tomboy growing up on the Wisconsin frontier in the 1860's. Full of adventure and courage, Caddie reflects not only the changes in America during that time but those of a young girl growing into womanhood. This book lends itself to a discussion of political and social change.

Themes
1. Family relationships
2. Cultural conflict
3. Native American-white relationships and English-American relationships
4. Sex-role stereotyping
5. Role of courage in the face of conflict

Literary Objectives
1. Recognize and evaluate character development
2. Analyze the elements of folklore and storytelling
3. Analyze the author's style

Companion Titles
1. *The Sign of the Beaver* - Elizabeth G. Speare (Native American-white relationships, role of courage in face of conflict, conflict of culture)
2. *Little House in the Big Woods* - Laura Ingalls Wilder (growing up on the frontier, family relationships)
3. *Matchlock Gun* - Walter Edmonds (growing up on the frontier, conflict of culture, family relationships)

Caddie Woodlawn
Author's Notes and Chapters 1–3

Vocabulary

virtues   irresolutely   piously   ominously   perilous
unfathomable   genial   reproachfully   disheveled   abolition

1. What attracted the author to her grandmother? Why did she want to write about her? How did the author know that her portrayal of her grandmother's family was accurate?

2. How does Carol describe her grandmother's personality?

3. Describe the Woodlawn trio.

4. What did the three children think of the Indians?

5. Why did the children cross the river?

6. What was Caddie and Indian Joe's relationship? How had it developed?

7. How did the Circuit Rider make Caddie feel? Why?

8. Why had Father encouraged Caddie to be a tomboy?

9. What was happening in the United States at the time of this story? What was Father's stance on the Civil War? Why?

10. Explain the quote, "The pigeons, like the Indians, were fighting a losing battle with the white man."

11. Which of the Woodlawn children are you most like? Explain.

Caddie Woodlawn
Chapters 4-8

Vocabulary
indignation   infamy   silhouette   haughty   barbarous
tumultuous   reverberated   indignation   pommel
contemptuously

1. How did Uncle Edmund get Caddie angry?

2. Why didn't Caddie want to take the silver dollar? What does this tell you about Caddie? Would you have felt the same way?

3. What happened to Nero? How did Caddie feel about this?

4. In what ways were the pioneer schools different from schools today?

5. Explain how Obediah had met his Waterloo.

6. How did the ice mishap change the winter for Caddie?

7. Explain the chain of events that occurred when Caddie tried to repair the circuit rider's clock. What do you think Caddie learned besides how clocks worked?

8. Explain the mystery of the clogs and breeches.

9. Did the story make the impression on the children that Father had wanted to make? Explain.

10. How did Father feel about his loss of the family fortune? How did Mother feel? If you were Caddie, how would you have felt?

11. Would Caddie be a different person if her grandfather had not been disinherited? How?

19

Caddie Woodlawn
Chapters 9-12

Vocabulary

miserly   inconsolable   obscurity   mutely   abstracted
indolent   treacherously   elation

1. What did the author mean by the boys' "fancies betrayed them into paper lace and true love knots?"

2. What did Caddie think about Tom getting Katie a store-bought valentine? Why?

3. How did Caddie feel about America?

4. Why was Caddie so upset when she received Uncle Edmund's letter?

5. What news did Melvin Kent bring? How did Mother and Father react differently to the news?

6. Why was the fear of Indians described as a disease? What other comparisons could be made?

7. What did Caddie overhear the men planning? What was her plan? Why?

8. What were some possible things that Caddie could have done? What would you have done if you were in Caddie's position?

9. What happened to Caddie when she went to the Indian camp? What feelings did she have throughout the experience?

10. What was Father's reaction to Caddie's escapade? How would your parents have reacted?

11. What was the reaction of Mother and the other children?

Caddie Woodlawn
Chapters 13–16

Vocabulary

confirmation	droning	protégés	resolute	consternation
ominously	gruesome	unaccountably	dubiously	guttural

1. What did Caddie do for Indian John while he was gone?

2. What were the children going to do with the scalp belt?

3. What happened to the Hankinson family?

4. How did Caddie "drive that awful lonesome look out of their eyes?"

5. How did Caddie get something for herself without buying anything?

6. How did Robert Ireton help the show?

7. How would the admission you might charge your friends compare to what the Woodlawn children received?

8. What had happened to Katie? Do you think the visit helped her? Why or why not?

9. What happened on the last day of school?

10. Up to this point, which of Caddie's adventures do you think is the best? Why?

Caddie Woodlawn
Chapters 17–20

Vocabulary

adage   sledge   anticlimax   refrain   aghast   vicissitude
rakishly

1. What did you think about the Pee-Wee story? What role did the Pee-Wee tale play in the Woodlawn family folklore? Does your family have any such stories?

2. Why was the arrival of the Little Steamer such a big event?

3. What was the big news that the Little Steamer brought? What news did the Circuit Rider bring? How do you suppose the settlers felt about the news?

4. Why did Caddie begin to think of Hetty differently? How does that account for her tattle-tale behavior?

5. What did Caddie think of Cousin Annabelle's letter? What would you have thought?

6. How did the boys save the school during the prairie fire? How do you think this incident changed the way the children and Miss Parker viewed Obediah?

7. What was cousin Annabelle like? How did the other children feel about her?

8. What did the nosegay incident tell you about Caddie, Hetty, and their changing relationship?

9. How did Caddie, Warren and Tom help Annabelle become uncivilized? What was her reaction? How did Caddie feel about this?

10. How would you have felt about having a cousin like Annabelle come to visit you?

Caddie Woodlawn
Chapters 21–24

Vocabulary

hoyden   irresolute   erstwhile   languishing   plaintive

1. What other trick did the children play on Annabelle? What chain of events did this start?

2. What was the Woodlawn family's unwritten law? Does your family have any such laws?

3. How was Caddie punished? What was her immediate reaction?

4. What did Father tell Caddie in the night? What did he want for her? What affect did this have?

5. What happened to the boys when Caddie learned to quilt?

6. What was the news Father shared with the family in the parlor?

7. How did Caddie feel about this opportunity?

8. How did the Woodlawn family decide their future?

9. Why did most of the family want to stay?

10. Why did Wisconsin seem dearer to Caddie now?

11. What travelers returned to the Woodlawn's home, and how was each greeted?

Caddie Woodlawn
Conclusion and Summary

1. Explain Caddie's quote in the last chapter, "Folks keep growing from one person into another all their lives." How did Caddie do this in the book? Do you agree with this quote?

2. Explain, "Life is just a lot of everyday adventures." Give examples to support your answers.

3. How was Indian John and Caddie's relationship a reciprocal one?

4. Compare your parent's expectations for you to those of Caddie's parents for her.

5. Tell whether or not you agree with the statement, "Money cannot buy happiness." Explain how Caddie's experience with her silver dollar confirms or contradicts this.

6. There are many heroes and heroines in this book. Identify three and tell how they are alike and different.

7. What was the crossroads in the lives of the Woodlawns? What did this incident do to their family relationships?

8. What was the relationship between Indians and white settlers? Discuss each group's feelings about the other.

9. In what ways might this book be considered patriotic? What ideals are shown?

10. What was the climax of the story? Was there more than one climax? Explain.

11. What things show that Caddie was sensitive? competitive? stubborn?

12. Would you have wanted to be Caddie's friend? Why?

Caddie Woodlawn
Activities

1. Research the history of steamboats as a means of transportation and communication. Make a detailed illustration or model of a boat like the Little Steamer.

2. Learn a folktale or tall tale like Tom's Pee-Wee tale and share it with the class. Provide some background information about the story you select.

3. Collect five to six pioneer songs and share them with the class either by singing them, playing them on an instrument, or playing a recording. Tell about the history of each one.

4. Be one of the characters from the book and present a monologue in which you tell about your feelings toward Caddie. Let the audience figure out who you are.

5. Make a poster or scrapbook of the highlights of the Civil War. Include 10 to 12 major events or turning points. Illustrate each event.

6. Make a board game that includes several of the happenings from the story as well as historic events and facts that are relevant to the story.

7. Research the conditions of Native Americans during the 1800's in the United States. Write a report that presents all the important events and viewpoints.

8. Pretend you are Caddie's penpal. Choose several incidents from the book and then write a letter to her telling her your reaction to her latest adventures. React to any feelings she might have shared with you.

9. Choose one of the skills that young girls were expected to learn when Caddie was young (quilting, embroidery, knitting, stitchery) and make a sample. Discuss your feelings about having different expectations and skills for boys and for girls.

The Door in the Wall
Marguerite de Angeli

Suggested Reading Levels
Grades 4–5

Biography
Marguerite de Angeli was born in Michigan in 1889 but grew up in Philadelphia. Since childhood, she had wanted to write and illustrate. She was also a very talented singer. Before embarking on a singing career, she met her husband, married and had six children and drew and wrote professionally. Her childhood provided models for her work. *The Door in the Wall* won the John Newbery Award in 1950. Mrs. de Angeli traveled to England to visit the churches, castles and inns that Robin experiences in *The Door in the Wall*. Her other works include *The Empty Barn,* and *Bright April*.

Synopsis
Historical Fiction
Set in medieval London, a young man named Robin finds himself struck by an illness that leaves him unable to do many things. Temporarily orphaned because of the war, Robin is cared for by Brother Luke, a monk at the St. Mark's hospice. This book gives a good view of the daily life of people in 13th century England and is an excellent source for teaching symbolism and theme. The vocabulary is difficult, but the message is easily interpreted.

Themes
1. Setting goals
2. Dealing with conflict and overcoming obstacles
3. Relationships between friends and parent–child

Literary Objectives
1. Identify and analyze the use of symbolism and theme
2. Identify the elements of historical fiction
3. Analyze character development
4. Analyze the relationship between plot and theme

Companion Titles
1. *Jonathan Livingston Seagull* – Richard Bach (dealing with conflict, setting goals)
2. *The Black Cauldron* – Lloyd Alexander (good verses evil)
3. *Freedom Train* – Dorothy Sterling (overcoming obstacles)

The Door in the Wall
Chapters 1–2

Vocabulary

putrid	breviary	priory	conduit	sedately	vexation
malady	grotesque	hospice	awry		

1. Why wasn't Robin with his parents? How would you have felt if your parents had left you when you were only ten years old?

2. What is the setting of the story? What clues are given?

3. What were Robin's parents expecting him to learn?

4. Why did Brother Luke come to help Robin?

5. What important advice did Brother Luke give Robin? What did it mean?

6. In your opinion, what kind of person is Robin? Describe his personality based on events from these chapters.

7. How do you suppose Robin felt when he found out that he had been left all alone? How did he feel about going to St. Mark's?

8. How did Robin pass the time at St. Mark's? Why was it so important to him?

9. What jobs did the monks have in the monastery?

10. What angered Robin? How was Robin feeling when it came time for his prayers?

11. Up to this point, how would things be different if it had taken place in the present?

The Door in the Wall
Chapters 3-4

Vocabulary

cloisters   acrid   weir   tonsure   fervently

1. How did Robin deal with his anger at the beginning of Chapter 3?

2. How could reading be a door in the wall for Robin?

3. Explain what Brother Luke meant when he said to Robin, "Weariness shall not give thee excuse for discouragement."

4. What feelings did Robin show in his letter to his father? How did Brother Luke feel about his words?

5. What happened when Robin and Brother Luke went fishing? How did Robin feel about this?

6. What kind of education was Robin receiving at the monastery? How did this compare to the education his father had planned for him? Which do you feel was best? Why?

7. What worried Robin about being lame?

8. How could crutches be a door in the wall for Robin?

9. What secret did Robin keep until work began on the crutches?

10. How was Robin improving, physically and emotionally? Do you think Brother Luke did a good job of planning experiences that would strengthen Robin's body, mind, and spirit? Explain.

The Door in the Wall
Chapters 5-6

Vocabulary

verger   minstrel   slatternly   farthing   roisterer

1. What message did Robin receive from his father?

2. How had Robin changed since he wrote to his father?

3. What problems did Robin and the group encounter on the first day's journey?

4. How did Robin feel about the trip so far?

5. At what kind of place did Robin stay the second night?

6. What plan did Robin overhear?

7. How did Robin save himself and his friends? What would you do in this situation?

8. Where did the group finally spend the night?

9. Give an example of Brother Luke's honesty and kindness.

10. Give an example of a descriptive phrase or passage that creates a vivid image for the reader.

11. In the first part of the book, Brother Luke explained how people got their last names. Think about Robin and what he is like and suggest several last names for him.

The Door in the Wall
Chapters 7–8

Vocabulary

caparison   cavalcade   marauding   esquire   covet
ingrate   largess   breached

1. Describe the fair at Wychwood Bec.

2. Why did the woods remind Robin of a cathedral?

3. How did Robin feel about meeting Sir Peter? Were his fears justified? Why?

4. What advice did Robin hear from Sir Peter?

5. What were the ways the castle could be conquered?

6. What was Robin's routine at his new home?

7. Explain Brother Luke's meaning when he spoke of a "crooked spirit" and "the measure of success; what we do with what we have."

8. What changes were occurring in Robin's personality and abilities?

9. What did John mean by "anyone can **not** do something?"

10. What happened in the fog?

11. Without reading ahead to the next chapter, suggest several things that could happen.

The Door in the Wall
Chapters 9-10

Vocabulary

bastion   cumbered   sacristan   ward   dais   catapult

1. What did Robin learn as he waited with the others inside the castle?

2. What problem occurred because there were more people in the castle?

3. What was Robin's plan?

4. What problems did Robin have to overcome in order to get to John?

5. What news did John-go-in-the-Wynd bring when he returned?

6. How was the town of Lindsay saved?

7. Why do you suppose Robin was willing to risk his life?

8. Put yourself in Robin's place and tell how you felt a) when you were returning to the castle with John, b) when John carried you through the town, c) when you were reunited with your parents, and d) when you were given the title of sir.

9. What was Robin celebrating at the Feast of Christmas?

10. Why was Robin given the title of "sir" by the king?

11. Explain Brother Luke's remark to Robin, "Thou has found the door in thy wall."

The Door in the Wall
Conclusion and Summary

1. Robin's personality changed in the book. Explain how. Who do you think helped Robin's personality change the most? Why?

2. Robin learned many things in the course of the book. Tell the five most important things he learned. Why do you think each was so important?

3. What do you think is in Robin's future? Be specific.

4. How did Robin's parents' expectations for him change after they learned of his illness? Explain your answer.

5. How was Robin strengthened (physically, spiritually, mentally, and emotionally) throughout the book? How was this accomplished?

6. What lessons did you learn that you can apply to your life? Apply the theme of a "door in the wall" from this book to your own life.

7. The "door" was used as a symbol in this story. What did it represent? What are some other symbols in this story? Explain how they were used.

8. What was the real conflict in this story? What obstacle did the main character have to overcome? Was it resolved or conquered? How?

9. What things (tangible and intangible) were most important to Robin? Which of these would also be important to you? Why?

10. Pretend this story is being written as a newspaper article. Write a headline and short answers to the questions who, what, where, when, and why. In what section of the newspaper would the story appear?

The Door in the Wall
Activities

1. Write an essay on the qualities that make a good parent (mother or father).
   Then tell about each of these characters and rate each as a parent to Robin:
   Brother Luke, Peter, Lindsay, and John de Bureford.

2. Write an ending chapter or epilogue for *The Door in the Wall*. This chapter
   should tell what happens to Robin and the other main characters in a few years
   after the end of the book.

3. Put the major events from the book into a sequenced timeline. Use words and
   pictures.

4. Write a diary from Robin's point of view about the two days when he saved the
   castle. Include his feelings and reasons for going.

5. How might this book have ended differently if Robin had not crossed the river?
   Write a new ending.

6. Make a model or floor plan of the monastery where Robin recovered or of Sir
   Peter's castle. Include important details from the book and from your research.

7. Prepare an oral or written report on the medieval period in Europe. In your
   report, explain social classes and the government of the period.

8. Make a mural, map, or diorama that shows the setting of this book.

9. Would this story make a good movie? Write a letter to a producer trying to
   convince him or her to make it into a movie. Tell about the three most exciting
   parts. Suggest a rating for the movie.

10. Pretend that you are the costume designer for the movie that is based on this
    book. Research medieval clothing and the make several drawings showing the
    clothes that will be worn by several of the characters.

Freedom Train
Dorothy Sterling

Suggested Reading Level
Grades 4-5

Biography
Dorothy Sterling was born in New York City on November 23, 1913. She married and had two children. Besides being a writer of historical books (particularly about the struggles for freedom of black Americans), she has written books and articles related to science and biology. *Freedom Train, The Story of Harriet Tubman* was published in 1959. Ms. Sterling has been a secretary, researcher, and free-lance writer in addition to being a published author.

Synopsis
Historical Biography
Freedom Train brings to life the real-life drama and personal experiences of the courageous Harriet Tubman and her accomplishments on the underground railroad and later during the Civil War. Dorothy Sterling gives the reader an intimate view of Harriet's motivations and feelings in this historically accurate biography. In this account of her life, Harriet is born a slave, but once free, she dedicates her life to securing freedom for all blacks.

Themes
1. Dignity of human beings
2. Importance and price of freedom
3. Significance of one person's attempt to change social conditions
4. Role of courage and conviction in overcoming obstacles

Literary Objectives
1. Identify and understand character development through action
2. Identify the elements of a biography
3. Analyze history presented through a biography

Companion Titles
1. *Sounder* – William Armstrong (price of freedom, injustice)
2. *The Cay* – Theodore Taylor (prejudice and racial harmony)
3. *Across Five Aprils* – Irene Hunt (price of freedom, impact of the past on the present
4. *The Pushcart War* – Joan Merrill (social conflict and change)
5. *The Sign of the Beaver* – Elizabeth George Speare (role of courage and conviction)
6. *The Door in the Wall* – Marguerite de Angeli (courage and overcoming obstacles)

Freedom Train
Chapters 1–3

Vocabulary

ration   resinous   reproach   despairingly   pestilence
liberation   abolitionist   sentinel

1. What was the setting of this story?

2. Why did Harriet run away from the big house? What does this incident tell you about her or her life?

3. What was Harriet like? Did she make a good slave girl? Why or why not?

4. How did Harriet get stronger? Explain both ways.

5. What role did music play in Harriet's life? How did she help others with her songs?

6. Explain Cudjoe's background. How had his past experiences affected his present life?

7. What idea was startling and puzzling to Harriet? Give some evidence that Cudjoe's remarks were true.

8. Who was Nat Turner? Did he do the **right** thing? How was he significant to Harriet?

9. How did the plantation owners try to "extinguish the slaves' capacity to see the light?" Why did they want to do this?

10. What kind of schooling did Harriet get? Was it appropriate?

Freedom Train
Chapters 4–5

Vocabulary
girth   cotillion   lustrous

1. Who told Harriet about the Underground Railroad? Why did this person and Harriet get along so well?

2. Explain how Harriet was hurt. What permanent damage was done?

3. How did the blow change her life?

4. How did Harriet view this new opportunity?

5. How did Harriet earn money?

6. How did her master's response when she inquired about buying her freedom make Harriet feel? Why do you think he wanted so much money for her?

7. Explain what a "free" negro was.

8. What problems did Harriet and John have?

9. Why did Harriet know she **must** run away? (Chapter 5)

10. What three adjectives would you use to describe Harriet? John? Master?

11. If you were in Harriet's place, what would you do?

Freedom Train
Chapters 6-9

Vocabulary

stolid   genial   devoid   unwittingly   ramshackle
insistent   somber   mechanically

1. How did Harriet and the Quaker lady converse? What precautions did they take?

2. Why did Harriet and her brothers turn back? Why did she finally go on her own?

3. Why did Harriet sleep soundly on the mossy ground for the first time in many months?

4. Explain how Harriet found her way by day and by night.

5. Tell about Harriet's experiences with both of the Hunn families. Why do you suppose they were willing to help runaway slaves?

6. What dangers did Harriet face? What, in your opinion, was her most threatening experience?

7. How did Harriet feel once she was in Pennsylvania?

8. What was Harriet's Christmas purchase? Why? In your opinion was her money well-spent? Explain.

9. Who was William Still? Why was he important to blacks?

10. Why did Still discourage Harriet from returning to her people? Why didn't it do any good?

Freedom Train
Chapters 10–12

Vocabulary
apprentices   pretensions   shrewdness   clamber   tremulous
exertion

1. How did Harriet help her sister? How did she help her brothers? Explain.

2. Why were these two trips less hazardous than future ones?

3. What had happened to John Tubman?

4. Describe Harriet's leadership qualities during an escape.

5. Explain the close call Harriet experienced during William Henry's escape.

6. Why wouldn't Harriet tell her mother her plans? How do you think her parents felt about her trips to free other slaves?

7. Explain how Harriet was a "Moses."

8. How did Harriet get money to rescue her parents?

9. How did Harriet free her parents?

10. If you could talk to Harriet's parents, what do you think they would say about their daughter?

Freedom Train
Chapters 13–16

Vocabulary

philanthropist	foray	secession	manacled	terminus
patriarchal	deluded	contraband		

1. How did the Underground Railroad change in the 1850's? How did these changes affect the lives of free runaways?

2. How did people help slaves who were trying to escape? What effect, in your opinion, did this have on Harriet and people like her?

3. Explain the significance of Harriet's quote, "They had the cold in their hearts; in you, it's not more than skin-deep."

4. Compare life in Maryland to life in Canada for Harriet's family.

5. What legends about Harriet came from the slaves? What did the slave owners think? What did you infer from the term "human livestock?"

6. What were the arguments on both sides of the slavery debate? What solutions were proposed? How did Harriet help the anti slavery cause?

7. How was Harriet viewed differently in the North and South? Explain the reasons why.

8. Explain John Brown's plan. How had slavery become a "state of war?" Why did he need Harriet's support? What were the effects of John Brown's raid?

9. Why was President Lincoln hesitant to use Negro soldiers? How was Harriet put to use?

Freedom Train
Chapters 17–20

Vocabulary
destitute   furlough   domestic   centenarians   suffragette
temperance   querulous

1. What were Harriet's duties (voluntary and assigned)?

2. What problems did she have to overcome? What rewards did she receive?

3. Give three ways Harriet knew "our time is coming." What did she mean by that?

4. Why and how did the freedmen celebrate January 1, 1863? What was the Emancipation Proclamation? How did it change warfare?

5. Explain one of Harriet's war triumphs. Why do you think she was so successful?

6. What inequity existed for black soldiers? What were Harriet's feelings about this?

7. What dilemma did Harriet face when trying to decide whether to go to Virginia with the women volunteers? What did this tell you about her character?

8. How did Harriet receive her war wound? What did the baggage car incident imply about the conductor's attitude? How did Harriet feel about this?

9. In what ways was Harriet's heart too big for her head? Why was it hard for her to save money?

10. How did Harriet continue to help other people?

Freedom Train
Conclusion and Summary

1. Explain how the baggage car incident was a reflection of people's hearts. What effect would this attitude have on the freedom of black Americans?

2. What three characteristics made Harriet a heroine? Give three adjectives that describe Harriet and explain each with an incident from the story.

3. What social and moral issues are raised in this book? What are your opinions on each?

4. Harriet Tubman spent all her adult life helping other people. She kept saying, "Our time is coming." Have the blacks gained equal rights in today's world? Why or why not? Use current events to support your answer.

5. In this biography, what do you think is the main idea or theme the author is trying to communicate? How is she successful in presenting this theme?

6. Was Harriet destined to be famous or extraordinary? What circumstances from her youth and early adulthood laid the foundation for her destiny?

7. If you could interview Harriet Tubman, what questions would you ask her?

8. Which person, in your opinion, had the greatest impact on Harriet? Explain how this person helped Harriet become a heroine.

9. What was the greatest tragedy of Harriet's life? What is the greatest tragedy of all blacks in our country? What was Harriet's greatest triumph? Why?

10. What lessons can be learned from this story that you could apply to your life?

11. What intangible ideas (freedom, love, determination, etc.) are shown in this book. How is each idea presented?

Freedom Train
Activities

1. Prepare an illustrated timeline of Harriet's accomplishments. Use this book to help you with the chronological order.

2. Research the life and contributions of one other famous abolitionists of the period (like Fredrick Douglass, Sojourner Truth, John Brown) or other civil rights leaders (like Martin Luther King, Jr.). Prepare a report (oral or written) comparing this person and his/her contributions and experiences with those of Harriet Tubman.

3. Prepare a historically accurate interview of Harriet Tubman, a reenactment of one event, or a first-person monologue. Write out a script and make your presentation as realistic as possible.

4. Make a map of the part of the United States that Harriet traveled through on the Underground Railroad and her missions during the Civil War.

5. Find text and/or recordings of several old spirituals that were sung by the slaves. Choose some to share with the class. Explain each one.

6. Choose a specific historical event or topic from this book (like John Brown's raid on Harper's Ferry, the Emancipation Proclamation, Nat Turner's rebellion, the Quakers, or the Anti-Slavery Society). Prepare an oral or written report on the topic.

7. Create a poem that memorializes Harriet Tubman and her efforts to free slaves and help other people.

8. Pretend that Harriet Tubman is still alive. Write a letter to her telling her how you feel about her achievements.

9. Write an eulogy for Harriet Tubman that emphasizes her life-time contributions.

Island of the Blue Dolphins
Scott O'Dell

Suggested Reading Level
Grades 4 – 5

Biography
    Scott O'Dell was born in California in 1903. He worked as a cameraman for a period of time. His love of nature is demonstrated in his work. Usually his books for children are told in first person by a young character. His strengths lie in his techniques of character development and point of view. *Island of the Blue Dolphins* was the winner of the Newbery Award in 1967. Other novels include *Sing Down the Moon*, and *Journey to Jericho*.

Synopsis
Realistic Fiction
    Karana was a Native American girl who had to learn to survive alone on the *Island of the Blue Dolphins*. She was left behind when her tribe abandoned the island, and she waited for years to be rescued. Karana was able to feed and protect herself. Finally help does arrive. The story is based on a true event.

Themes
1. Survival in the wild
2. Human interaction with nature
3. Courage in overcoming obstacles

Literary Objectives
1. Analyze the character development, symbols
2. Identify qualities of a Newbery Award winner
3. Identify author's style by comparison of his other works
4. Identify and analyze point of view, simile, and imagery

Companion Titles
1. *The Sign of the Beaver* – Elizabeth G. Speare (survival in the wilderness, conflict of culture, courage in overcoming obstacles)
2. *The Cay* – Theodore Taylor (survival in the wild, interaction of man and nature)
3. *Sing Down the Moon* – Scott O'Dell (courage in the face of conflict, author comparison)

Island of the Blue Dolphins
Chapters 1-2

Vocabulary

cormorant   kelp   mesa   parley   leagues   idle
dunes

1. The author used similes to describe the Aleut ship. To what did he compare the red ship with two sails? Make your own simile about a ship.

2. What metaphor did Ramo use to describe the sea? How did this help you visualize the sea?

3. Why didn't Karana rush away when she saw the ship? What does that tell you about her character?

4. What surprised Karana about her father's encounter with the Russian? Why?

5. What did the Russians propose?

6. What decision did the Chief and Captain make? Was this a good one for the island people?

7. Why did the Captain want to come ashore immediately?

8. Why was the island called the Island of the Blue Dolphins?

9. What was the Chief's warning to his villagers?

10. What good fortune did the villagers have?

Island of the Blue Dolphins
Chapters 3–5

Vocabulary

carcass   surged   shirkers   perish   portioned   abalones
decreed   bale

1. How did Karana feel about the hunters? Why?

2. What was the Chief afraid the Aleuts would do? Why was he cautious?

3. What clues told the islanders the Aleuts were preparing to leave?

4. What happened between the Aleuts and the Islanders when the Aleuts were ready to leave?

5. How did Karana explain what happened to her father?

6. What effect did the battle have on the islanders?

7. Describe the new chief. What changes did he propose?

8. What problems existed in the village?

9. What was the real cause of the unrest? What sickness came over the island?

10. When spring came, what did Kimki decide to do? Why?

Island of the Blue Dolphins
Chapters 6–8

Vocabulary

shrouded   vain   forlorn   yucca   gorge   lair
nettles   rites

1. What did Matasaip mean by "there are other more important things to ponder?"

2. How did the islanders plan to deal with the Aleuts if they came back? Was it a good plan?

3. What news did the ship bring? How did the islanders feel about this?

4. What did Karana pack? What would you pack if you were in her position?

5. Why did the Islanders have trouble getting aboard ship? Why were the white men unwilling to turn back?

6. How did Ramo and Karana get separated from the other islanders? What feelings did Karana have?

7. How did Ramo feel about staying on the island with Karana?

8. Why didn't Karana want to let Ramo go to the cove by himself?

9. What happened to Ramo? How did this change events greatly?

10. What did Karana vow to do?

Island of the Blue Dolphins
Chapters 9–11

Vocabulary
omen   brackish

1. What idea had Karana come to grips with at the beginning of Chapter 9?

2. What jobs did Karana see as necessary to begin?

3. What dilemma did Karana face in regards to weapons? What do you think she should have done and why?

4. What did the jewels stand for to Karana? What did she do with them?

5. What weapons did Karana produce for her protection? How did she know how to make them?

6. Why did Karana now feel lonely when she had not before?

7. Why was Karana willing to risk the dangers of the sea?

8. What problems did Karana face as she set out with the canoe? What feelings did she experience?

9. What did the dolphins symbolize?

10. How did Karana feel about returning to the island? How had her feelings changed?

11. Once she knew she was destined to stay on the island, what did she decide to do?

Island of the Blue Dolphins
Chapters 12 – 13

Vocabulary

sandspit   sinew   gruel   wary

1. How did Karana use her resources wisely?

2. What was the Indian legend about the trees?

3. What foods did Karana eat? Which sound appetizing to you? Why?

4. What evidence do you have that Karana was resourceful?

5. How did the dogs continue to threaten Karana?

6. What characteristics did Karana exhibit at this point in the book?

7. Why did she want to kill a sea elephant? What dangers did this present?

8. How did superstition and tradition affect Karana's life?

9. The author used many descriptive phrases or passages to tell about the sea elephants. Find at least three.

10. Why were the bulls fighting? What did this do to Karana's plans?

11. The author often used similes to help the reader visualize the events. Find three examples.

Island of the Blue Dolphins
Chapters 14-19

Vocabulary

lobe   venturing   pitch   singe   flank   flail

1. What happened to Karana on her way to the spring? What did she do?

2. Why had the dogs not been a problem in earlier years on the island?

3. What was Karana's plan for killing the dogs?

4. How was Karana's relationship with the dog changing?

5. What plans was Karana making for the future?

6. What purpose did Rontu serve for Karana? Why was he important to her?

7. What happened with Rontu and the wild dog? What did Rontu's fight mean to him and the other dogs?

8. Who were Tainor and Lurai? How did they become Karana's friends?

9. How did Karana try to catch the giant devilfish? What happened? How would you rate her success?

10. What doubts and fears might have run through Karana's mind while she was trying to kill the devilfish?

Island of the Blue Dolphins
Chapters 20–Author's Notes

Vocabulary

giddy   reproachfully   fledglings   quiver   vanquished

1. What did Karana find in the black cave? Why did she vow not to return?

2. What did Karana do when she saw the Aleut ship? Why?

3. What did Karana do while she hid from the Aleuts?

4. Who was Tutok? How did she make Karana feel?

5. How did Tutok and Karana become friends?

6. How had Karana's ideas about animals changed from that of her family?

7. How did Karana catch the young dog? Why do you think she wanted another dog?

8. What happened the day Karana went to the sandspit? How did Karana feel about the visitors?

9. How did Karana feel about leaving the island? What would you have thought?

10. What had happened to Karana's people?

Island of the Blue Dolphins
Conclusion and Summary

1. List three characteristics or traits of Karana. Give examples from the book as evidence. What characteristic do you think was the most important?

2. Tutok was an Aleut, and the Aleuts had killed Karana's people. How could she and Karana have become friends?

3. Explain how Karana's attitude about nature stayed the same and also changed in the course of the book.

4. Rescue means to save or free from danger, imprisonment or evil. Did Karana need rescuing? Why or why not?

5. In the author's notes, the reader found out that Karana never became friendly with the people in her new home. Why do you think this was?

6. Karana got along very well on her island. Why did she leave?

7. Karana wisely used her natural resources. Give examples of this.
   Why was it important then and now?

8. There were several situations involving conflict that Karana faced throughout the book. List several of these and tell how she overcame each.

9. Who tells this story? How would it be different if it were told from another point of view?

10. Karana learned to be independent. On the other hand, she did show a need for interdependence and relationships. Find examples of this need.

11. What did you learn about history, geography, and nature from reading this book?

Island of the Blue Dolphins
Activities

1. Karana developed many skills while on the island. List some of the skills and determine how you might be able to learn these particular skills today.

2. Make a map of the island using descriptions from the book.

3. Choose an exciting portion of the novel and rewrite it from another point of view.

4. Create titles for each chapter and draw at least three illustrations for events in the story.

5. Read *Zia* or another survival story and compare to this story.

6. Research seal elephants, dolphins, sea otters or squid and share your information in a written or oral report.

7. Pretend that you are a newspaper reporter and write an article about Karana's arrival at Mission Santa Barbara and her life on the island.

8. This story was made into a movie. Create a poster to advertise the movie. Use descriptive words that will make people want to see the movie.

9. Pretend you are the producer who is going to make this story into a movie. Choose at least ten incidents to be included in the movie. Out of that list, choose one and create a story board showing the important scenes and actions.

10. Make a diorama of Karana's living area. Include details from the book.

11. Make a drawing and a brief description of each animal on Karana's island.

The Lion, The Witch and the Wardrobe
C. S. Lewis

Suggested Reading Level
Grades 4-6

Biography
  C. S. Lewis was a British scholar, critic and author who was born in 1898 and died in 1963. He was best known for his novels that had religious or moral themes, but he also wrote children's stories and critical works. Other books in the Chronicles of Narnia include *Prince Caspian, The Voyage of the Dawn, Treader, The Silver Chair, The Horse and His Boy, The Magician's Nephew,* and the *Last Battle.* C. S. Lewis was also a professor of medieval and Renaissance English at Cambridge University.

Synopsis
Fantasy

  When four children are moved from London to the countryside home of a Professor during World War II, they have no idea of the adventures behind a wardrobe door in a land called Narnia. In Narnia they meet the White Witch who has made it always winter and never spring, and Aslan who, with their help can free the land. This is a book that can be read and interpreted on several levels.

Themes
1. Loyalty
2. Good versus evil

Literary Objectives
1. Identify and analyze symbolism
2. Examine character development
3. Identify themes
4. Identify elements of a story

Companion Titles
1. *Little Prince* – Antoine de Saint Exupery (meaning of life, relationships)
2. *Black Cauldron* – Lloyd Alexander (good versus evil)
3. *A Wrinkle in Time* – Madeleine L'Engle (good versus evil, relationships)

The Lion, the Witch and the Wardrobe
Chapter 1

Vocabulary

wireless   wardrobe

1. Why did the children leave London to come to the old Professor's home?

2. What did Peter mean when he said that they had fallen on their feet?

3. Describe the Professor's home.

4. Explain what happened when Lucy entered the wardrobe.

5. What do you know about the four children at this point in the story?

6. If you were in Lucy's place, would you have done what she did or would you have gone back for your brothers and sister so they could go with you?

7. Describe the faun.

The Lion, the Witch and the Wardrobe
Chapters 2–3

Vocabulary

inquisitive   melancholy   hoax   elder   jeered   spiteful
Pax   sulking   sledge

1. What was the faun's name and where did he say they were?

2. What did Mr. Tumnus say he had never seen before? What does this mean in our language?

3. Describe the home of Mr. Tumnus.

4. How did Mr. Tumnus entertain Lucy?

5. What terrible thing did Mr. Tumnus plan to do? Why had he planned to do this?

6. Why did he let Lucy go?

7. What spell had the White Witch cast over the land of Narnia?

8. Mr. Tumnus asked for a remembrance of Lucy. What was it?

9. How did time in Narnia compare to time where the children came from?

10. How did Edmund happen into the wardrobe?

11. What problem occurred for Lucy when she tried to take the other children to Narnia with her?

12. Describe what Edmund saw when the sledge came into sight.

The Lion, the Witch and the Wardrobe
Chapters 4-5

Vocabulary

dominion   mantle   inquisitive   consideration   reliable
logic

1. What was unusual about the Turkish Delight?

2. What did Edmund tell the Queen that interested her greatly?

3. Tell what promises the Queen made to Edmund if he would come to her castle. To get these promised rewards what was required of Edmund?

4. By the end of Chapter 4, Edmund has some complicated feelings about the Queen. What are these mixed feelings?

5. What mean and spiteful thing did Edmund decide to do at the beginning of Chapter 5?

6. Why did Susan and Peter decide to confide in the Professor?

7. What did the Professor point out to the children about Lucy, reality, and time?

8. How did the four children end up in the wardrobe together?

The Lion, the Witch and the Wardrobe
Chapters 6–8

Vocabulary

camphor   wrenched   fraternizing   token   stratagem
prophecy   treacherous

1. What did the children discover about Edmund when they got to Narnia? How did he give himself away?

2. What techniques did Edmund use to try to sway Peter to his side?

3. How did Mr. Beaver show that he was to be trusted?

4. What happened to the children when Aslan's name was mentioned?

5. What was Edmund feeling when he recognized the two small hills?

6. According to Mr. Beaver, what had probably happened to Mr. Tumnus?

7. Explain who Aslan was.

8. Why were the four children in danger?

9. How did Mr. Beaver know that Edmund had gone to the White Witch?

10. What did Mrs. Beaver say was the only way to save all four children?

The Lion, the Witch and the Wardrobe
Chapters 9–11

Vocabulary

turret   ventured   satyrs   centaur   lithe   eerie
repulsive   gluttony   vicious

1. What excuse did Edmund use for going to the White Witch?

2. Describe the courtyard of the White Witch's palace.

3. What was the White Witch's reaction to Edmund's news?

4. What was the first clue that the White Witch's power was crumbling? Why was her power crumbling?

5. What gifts and advice did each child receive?

6. How were things different than Edmund had thought they would be?

7. What made Edmund feel sorry for someone besides himself?

8. What happened as the White Witch sped toward the Stone Table? What did this mean?

The Lion, the Witch and the Wardrobe
Chapters 12-13

Vocabulary

schemes   crimson   rampart   pavillion   velveted
sceptre   renounced

1. Describe the Stone Table.

2. How did the children feel when they met or saw Aslan?

3. What was Peter's response to Aslan's question? Why did he say that?

4. What almost happened to Edmund? How was he rescued?

5. What happened to the Witch as Edmund was rescued?

6. Write a paragraph telling what you think Aslan said to Edmund after his rescue.

7. What did the White Witch say was the Deep Magic?

8. What did the White Witch ask Aslan for?

The Lion, the Witch and the Wardrobe
Chapters 14–15

Vocabulary
siege   groped   dismay   enrage   rabble   whet
vile   incantation   battlements

1. For what did Peter have to prepare?

2. What did the girls do for Aslan on his journey?

3. Why did Aslan surrender to the White Witch?

4. What did the White Witch say to Aslan at the end of Chapter 14?

5. What did the girls do when the evil ones left? How did they feel?

6. What happened to the Stone Table? How?

7. What magic was deeper than Deep Magic?

The Lion, the Witch and the Wardrobe
Chapters 16–17

Vocabulary
prodigious   ransacking   bay   din   solemn   alliance
foreboding

1. To what does the author compare the lion statue coming to life? How is this effective?

2. How did Aslan and his companion prepare for war?

3. What pleased the other lion? Why?

4. How was Edmund the hero? Why was it important that he be the hero?

5. What did the cordial do for Edmund?

6. What did Aslan need to remind Lucy of?

7. Were the children good rulers of Narnia? Why or why not? What were some of the things they did?

8. How were the children referred to in Narnia?

9. What did the Professor say about Narnia?

The Lion, the Witch and the Wardrobe
Conclusion and Summary

1. Identify three morals in this story. Do you agree with them? Explain.

2. What weakness did the White Witch use to get Edward's help? How is that a problem for all people?

3. Should Edmund know of Aslan's sacrifice for him? Why or why not?

4. Tell about a time or event that caused you to act or feel the way one of the children did in this story.

5. What was the Professor's philosophy about public education? Do you agree?

6. What lessons did Edmund learn? What wisdoms did Peter already have?

7. Do the children actually make a difference in this story or does Aslan need them to act on his behalf? How would the story be different if one child had behaved differently?

8. What examples of the White Witch's heartlessness can you find in the book? Did her character have any good in it?

9. The climax is the turning point or the most exciting part. What was the climax of this story?

10. In addition to a climax, most stories have a setting (time and place), a problem or conflict and an ending (usually comes after the climax.) Does this story have these parts? Briefly describe each one.

11. This book can be interpreted on a variety of levels. Identify four symbols in the book and explain each one.

The Lion, the Witch and the Wardrobe
Activities

1. Rewrite an event from the story from Edmund's point of view.

2. Make a travel brochure for Narnia. Use names of places in the book and descriptive words to make Narnia sound inviting.

3. Write a poem about Aslan, Narnia, or the children.

4. Design a mobile that includes characters and settings from the book.

5. Draw a map or mural of Narnia.

6. Make a game that includes places and events from this story.

7. Using one to two sentences for each, summarize each chapter.

8. Write a script of a scene from the book and with others act it out for the class.

9. Write a three paragraph essay. In the first paragraph write a summary of the book. In the second paragraph write an in-depth summary of what you think was the most interesting part of the book. In the third paragraph write why you feel that was the most interesting section.

10. How is this book an allegory of Christianity? Share your ideas in an essay.

11. Design a flag or banner for Narnia that includes the name, a motto, and at least one thing that is special about it. Make it attractive.

The Midnight Fox

Betsy Byars

Suggested Reading Level
Grades 4–5

Biography
Betsy Byars was born in 1928 in North Carolina, and graduated from Queens College. She now lives in South Carolina but has traveled throughout the United States. This prolific writer uses real life incidents on which to base her stories. Most of the time she writes in the winter and works with her husband in the summer on their glider. As a mother of four, she began writing books for her children as her family was growing up. She won the coveted Newbery Medal for *The Summer of the Swans*. Other works include *Trouble River*, *The House of Wings*, *The Winged Colt of Casa Mia*, and *The 18th Emergency*. Techniques used in her writing to enhance her stories are irony, strong character development, imagery, and conflict.

Synopsis
Tom is an only child who feels sorry for himself when his parents leave him with Uncle Fred and Aunt Millie on the farm while they go to Europe for the summer. Tom is resistant to trying new things, but as he adapts to his rural environment he learns a lot about himself and life in general. The focal point is his discovery of a rare black fox that he watches from a distance and then is forced to save through a series of heroic acts. Betsy Byars gives a sensitive portrait of an insecure child with many fears who learns to depend on his own resources as he matures.

Themes
1. Growing up
2. Development of friendships and family relationships
3. Human interaction with nature

Literary Objectives
1. Analyze the character development and conflicts
2. Identify and analyze the use of flashbacks, humor and irony

Companion Titles
1. *The Door in the Wall* – Marguerite de Angeli (growing up, relationships with family and friends)
2. *The Black Cauldron* – Lloyd Alexander (growing up, development of friendships, self–confidence)
3. *The Summer of the Swans* – Betsy Byars (growing up, author's style)

The Midnight Fox
Bad News – Abandoned

Vocabulary

figs   sarcastic   loathe   excelled   galvanized

1. What happens in the first two paragraphs that separates them from the rest of Chapter 1?

2. What were Tom's two clearest memories of the visit to the farm?

3. How did Tom react to going to the farm? Why?

4. How did Tom's mother and father act toward his desire not to go to the farm? Were they understanding of his position? How did each one make Tom feel?

5. What were some of the bad things Tom imagined would happen at the farm?

6. What would Tom miss most by being on the farm?

7. How was Tom different from his parents? What problems did this create for him?

8. If you were Tom's parents, how might you help him look more positively at the farm experience?

9. Why, in Tom's opinion, did his relatives want him to come to the farm? What kind of reception had he envisioned?

10. Tom tried successfully to stay in control. What did that mean? Was this his usual behavior? Why was he disappointed?

The Midnight Fox
Stranger – Hazeline

Vocabulary

sullen   assured   adaptable   demolished   incidentally
awesome

1. What preconceived ideas did Aunt Millie have about boys? Did these fit Tom?

2. What was the Petie Burkis Special? If you could invent a food, what would it be like? Name your creation.

3. Did Tom care about Aunt Millie's feelings? How do you know?

4. What was Tom's biggest problem?

5. Describe Tom's first days on the farm. How did he really feel about being there?

6. How did Tom first see the black fox?

7. Describe the black fox. Why was Tom so impressed by it?

8. Why didn't Tom tell Petie about the fox in his letter?

9. Give two reasons why Tom didn't tell anyone about the black fox.

10. What did Hazeline tell Tom about the neighbor and the fox? How did Tom feel about this news?

11. How did Tom's feelings about the fox differ from other people on the farm?

The Midnight Fox
Discovery at the Farm – The Search

Vocabulary
impulse   reluctantly   ritual   ravine   pigment
resolution   disgruntled

1. What does Tom's account of discovering a new color tell you about him?

2. Tom watched the black fox catch a mouse. Why was he so fascinated?

3. Why did Tom compare his fierce desire to follow the fox to Petie Burkis and Monopoly? What happened when he followed the fox?

4. Why could Tom talk to Hazeline?

5. What did Uncle Fred tell Tom about black foxes?

6. Describe Tom's search for the den. What did he see at the den?

7. Why did Tom decide never to go back to the den?

8. What hints does the author give you about what is going to happen later in the story?

9. Tom made up many imaginary experiences. Describe one. Do you have any favorite fantasies? How do they compare to Tom's?

The Midnight Fox
Tragedy Begins – Unwilling Hunter

Vocabulary

thrashing   tragedy   divert   laxity   impetuous
animation   quarrelsome

1. How was Tom changing? What made him feel so good?

2. Why was Aunt Millie upset? How did Uncle Fred react?

3. What was the tragedy that Tom feared? How did this fear compare to his other fears?

4. What dilemma did this present for Tom?

5. Why couldn't Hazeline help Tom?

6. Tom wished he could have used the magic word "Tacooma" or call upon Hercules to help, but he couldn't. What did he mean when he said his story would end with "a runny nose and wet eyes?" Invent a magic word you could use.

7. How did Uncle Fred feel about hunting?

8. Uncle Fred was a good hunter. List several of his actions that were evidence of his skill.

9. Why was Tom going along with Uncle Fred?

The Midnight Fox
The Den – A Memory

Vocabulary

intensity   secluded   bellowing   cowering   quavering
assuring   perilous

1. Tom knew how the baby fox felt. How did it feel? How did Tom know?

2. How was Uncle Fred going to catch the black fox?

3. When Tom woke up in the middle of the night, what did he do?

4. Why was this action heroic for Tom? What would you have done in a similar situation? Knowing what you are afraid of, what would be a heroic action for you?

5. Why did Tom go to the front door and ring the bell?

6. What was Uncle Fred's reaction to what Tom did? What was Aunt Millie's reaction?

7. How can you explain his aunt and uncle's reaction when it seemed they were so intent on killing the fox?

8. Why did Tom think Uncle Fred and Aunt Millie were the nicest people he had ever met?

9. How did Tom remember his summer on the farm?

10. Do you think Tom was the same and his relationships with other people were the same when he went back home? Explain.

The Midnight Fox
Conclusion and Summary

1. Memories are sometimes hazy and sometimes crystal clear. Explain how Tom's memory of the farm could be both.

2. Tom matured during his summer on the farm. How did he change? What, in your opinion, was the most important thing he learned?

3. Petie and Tom had a strong friendship. What was it like? What made their relationship a good one?

4. Why did Tom have trouble relating to adults (parents, aunt, uncle) in the first half of the book. Did this change? If so, how and why?

5. What did the fox symbolize in Tom's life? Why was it so important to him?

6. Explain how these themes or topics are dealt with in this book. Give examples.
   -growing up   -freedom
   -relationships and friendships   -survival

7. What was the climax of this story? Why was it the most exciting part? How did you feel at this point?

8. This story did not have a great deal of action or adventure. Much of the movement of the plot was really in Tom's maturation. How did the author make the book interesting?

9. Choose something from the book that made you laugh. Explain how the author used one of these techniques to make it humorous.
   -vivid description   -conflict between characters
   -exaggeration   -surprise
   -word play

10. What is the author saying about nature in this book? Do you agree?

The Midnight Fox
Activities

1. Do some research on foxes. Tell about their characteristics, habits, habitats, and other interesting facts in a written report or oral report.

2. Make a mural or map of the farm where Tom spent his summer. Label each significant spot. Include a key.

3. Write a collection of news articles about Tom's actual experiences or about his imagined experiences on the farm. Provide interesting headlines.

4. Prepare a summer reading list for Tom of at least ten books. Include fiction and nonfiction. List books that might give him information or might help him learn a lesson. Use proper bibliographical form and write a brief annotation telling how each particular book might have helped him.

5. Make a filmstrip or roller movie summarizing *The Midnight Fox*. Choose fifteen to twenty scenes to illustrate and write a script that will entice others to read the book.

6. Make a collection of poems about foxes or nature. Illustrate each poem and copy it on unlined paper. Make a cover and table of contents. Choose one to read aloud with expression.

7. Pretend you are Tom and make a time capsule for your summer on the farm. Explain the significance of each item in the capsule.

8. Write a letter from Tom to his aunt and uncle, thanking them for being able to stay with them and expressing all those things about his summer that he wanted to say but didn't.

9. Make a word collage that expresses your ideas about nature.

Dear Mr. Henshaw

Beverly Cleary

Suggested Reading Level
Grades 3-5

Biography
Beverly Cleary was born in 1916 in Oregon. She served as a librarian for some time. She is an extremely prolific writer of children's books and has won many awards. She attributes much of her feelings about books to the importance her mother placed on books, reading, and libraries. Ms. Cleary won the Newbery Honor Award in 1978 for *Ramona and Her Father* and the Newbery medal for Dear *Mr. Henshaw* in 1984.

Synopsis
Realistic Fiction

In this heart-touching story, Leigh learns to deal with several problems that young readers realistically have to face. He confronts loneliness associated with being the new boy in school and also from having to spend long periods alone at home as his mother works to provide a living for the two of them. He wrestles with his mixed feelings about his father who never calls or comes to see him. He learns how to solve problems, how to be a friend, and how to make progress toward his goal of being a writer. While the reading in this story is easy, the situations and feelings that are presented will provide opportunities for thought-provoking discussions.

Themes
1. Overcoming obstacles
2. Growing up
3. Family relationships
4. Loneliness
5. Adjusting to new environments

Literary Objectives
1. Character analysis
2. Elements of a story
3. Point of view

Companion Titles
1. *James and the Giant Peach* – Roald Dahl (overcoming obstacles)
2. *Soup an Me* – Robert Newton Peck (growing up)
3. *Otherwise Known as Sheila the Great* – Judy Blume (growing up, family relationships)
4. *Henry Huggins* – Beverly Cleary (growing up, family conflict, development of responsibility)

Dear Mr. Henshaw

May 12 – December 1

Vocabulary

refining   disgusted   duplex   loner

1. Why did Leigh begin writing to Mr. Henshaw?

2. What tips did Mr. Henshaw give Leigh about becoming a writer?

3. Why does Leigh feel he is the "mediumest" boy in class? Do you get the idea that he felt this was good or bad?

4. Describe Leigh's family, his parents' jobs, and how he feels about the jobs his parents have.

5. What does Leigh mean when he says about school, "If I hang in, I'll get out"?

6. What bothers Leigh?

7. What, according to Leigh's answer in number ten, did Leigh want most?

8. What do you think Mr. Henshaw's questions were designed to do?

9. What kind of a person do you think Mr. Henshaw is?

10. How do you know that Mr. Henshaw cared about children?

11. How did Leigh feel about the questions Mr. Henshaw sent? Did his feelings change any as he answered them?

73

Dear Mr. Henshaw
December 4 – December 21

Vocabulary

gondola   canape   partition   halyard

1. Leigh seemed to be angry with Mr. Henshaw for asking him to answer all his questions. We find out later, however, that he is really angry about other things. Why is Leigh really angry?

2. If Leigh wrote a story, why might it be titled The Great Lunchbag Mystery?

3. Who is Mr. Fridley and how did he help Leigh?

4. Why does Leigh say, "It's nice to have someone notice me"?

5. What made Leigh decide to write in a diary? How did he begin each entry and what made him decide to begin this way?

74

Dear Mr. Henshaw
December 22 – January 9

Vocabulary

snitch   foil   pseud. (pseudonym)   fictitious

1. Why doesn't Leigh tell his teacher that someone is stealing his lunch? What would you have done in a similar situation?

2. What is Leigh's plan to foil the lunchbag thief after Christmas vacation?

3. What was Leigh's memory of Christmas the year before?

4. Why did Leigh remember the story about the shoe fondly?

5. In what two ways was Leigh's Christmas gift from his dad special?

6. What does Leigh's mom mean when she says her friend Katy "has a heart as big as a football stadium"? What other analogy could be used to describe her?

7. "Keep your nose clean" is an idiom. What does it mean?

8. What was Mr. Fridley's suggestion about the disappearing food? How did Leigh's first attempt work?

9. How do you think Leigh's mom was feeling about her life as a single parent?

Dear Mr. Henshaw
January 12 – February 9

Vocabulary

nuisance   wrath   tournament   mildew   pride
mimeographed   molesting

1. Leigh decided to write to Mr. Henshaw again instead of putting his thoughts in his diary. Why did he decide to do this?

2. What in *Begger Bears* reminded him of his own family? What did he worry about?

3. How did Leigh describe Mr. Fridley on January 20th? What did this description mean? Can you think of any other words that would give the same idea?

4. Leigh seems to have a lot of feelings (some of which are conflicting) about his father. What are these feelings?

5. In what ways was Leigh's phone call with his father difficult for him?

6. How did Leigh's mom help him after the phone call? What did she say about the ocean? What in your life has the same soothing effect when things are bothering you?

7. In what ways was Leigh's mother a victim of circumstance? In what ways was she taking control of her life?

8. When Mr. Fridley spoke with Leigh on February 6th he gave him some good advice. What was the advice and how did it change Leigh?

9. Between February 7th and the 9th Leigh had several different feelings. What were these feelings? How would you have felt if you were in his shoes?

Dear Mr. Henshaw
February 15 – March 31

1. When Leigh was stuck on an ending for his story he wrote to Mr. Henshaw. What advice did Mr. Henshaw give him? Was it helpful? Why of why not?

2. There were several changes in Leigh's life because of the lunch box alarm. What were they and were they positive or negative changes?

3. After all his work Leigh decided that he didn't really want to catch the lunch box thief. Why? Do you agree with his thinking?

4. What problems did Leigh have deciding what to write? Why was it important to him that he do well in the contest? Why did Leigh finally decide to write about his dad?

5. Leigh says, "It helps to have a friend." What does he mean?

6. How did Leigh feel about not winning first or second place in the Young Writers' Yearbook contest? What did he think about those kids who said they would never write again?

7. How did Leigh happen to have lunch with Angela Badger?

8. What things did she say to him that made him feel so pleased about himself?

9. What one question did Leigh ask Angela Badger? What was her answer?

10. In the last chapter of the book Leigh's father came by for a visit. Leigh had changed in many ways since the beginning of the book. What were some of the changes you noticed in him?

11. Leigh missed Bandit. Why then didn't he keep him when offered the opportunity?

Dear Mr. Henshaw
Conclusion and Summary

1. Mr. Fridley helped Leigh more than once in the story. In what ways did he help?

2. Why did Leigh go to the butterfly trees the second time? Did it help him? Do you have a similar place that you go to? Describe it.

3. What ways did Leigh try to foil the lunchbag thief? How did Leigh feel about the lunchbag thief by the end of the book? How do you know?

4. What were Leigh's problems during the book? How did he deal with each of them?

5. Throughout the book Leigh had many conflicting feelings about his father. What were they? What did Leigh understand about his father by the end of the book?

6. Was this the best ending for the book? Why or why not?

7. What does the last sentence of the book mean? "I felt sad and a whole lot better at the same time."

8. Did you learn anything from any of the characters that would help you in your life? If so, what?

9. What part was 1) the most humorous, 2) the saddest, 3) the most exciting, 4) the part you liked best?

10. Write three paragraphs about the changes in Leigh from the beginning to the end of the book. In paragraph one describe his personality at the beginning of the book. In paragraph two describe his personality at the end of the book. In paragraph three explain what happened to make these changes take place.

11. Describe Leigh's personality. What characteristics do you admire?

Dear Mr. Henshaw
Activities

1. Choose four of Mr. Henshaw's questions for Leigh and answer them about yourself.

2. Leigh describes his bedroom as his private place. Is there a place you like to go to think in private? If there is, describe it using as many senses as possible. If there isn't, think of one that you wish you had and describe it.

3. Keep a diary for a week. See if it helps you in any way.

4. In a small cooperative learning group, make a lunch box alarm.

5. Write a poem (haiku or cinquain) about the butterfly trees or about some special natural place you enjoy visiting.

6. Make a map that shows all the places mentioned in the book. Use reference books to find one interesting fact about each place.

7. Choose a favorite author and write a letter to him or her. Tell what you especially like about his/her books and ask any questions you would like to have answered.

8. Leigh shared his feelings about his parents in his diary. Write a diary entry or a letter to one or both of your parents in which you share your feelings about them and tell what you especially appreciate and/or admire.

9. Make a drawing of the butterfly grove based on the author's description.

10. This book showed some of the problems that young people have to deal with. Make a collage, a poem or some other creative project that illustrates these and some other problems that are typical for people your age.

From the Mixed-up Files of Mrs. Basil E. Frankweiler

Elaine L. Konigsburg

Suggested Reading Level
Grades 4-5

Biography

Elaine Konigsburg authored and illustrated *From the Mixed-up Files of Mrs. Basil E. Frankweiler*. This novel won the Newbery award and was developed into a movie. Ms. Konigsburg was born in New York but grew up in Pennsylvania. She received a masters degree in Chemistry and taught for a while before starting her family. Once her children entered school, she began writing. Her books show an understanding of young people, because her former students and own children served as models for characters. A few of her other titles include *Jennifer, Hecate, Macbeth, William McKinley, and Me, Elizabeth; George; About the B'Nai Bagles;* and *Altogether, One At A Time*.

Synopsis
Realistic Fiction

Claudia is very unhappy with her life at home and decides to plan a get-away. Her thrifty younger brother, Jamie, saves his money and will prove to be useful in the runaway plan. Claudia wants her parents to miss her and realize how important she is to them. When the two arrive at the Metropolitan Museum of Art, they set up a schedule and plan. Claudia finds an intriguing art piece and will not return home until she finds the designer. This leads her to more involvement and the introduction to Mrs. Frankweiler. Mrs. Frankweiler helps Claudia find out about the statue and more about herself.

Themes
1. Family conflict
2. Coping with unique talents and gifts
3. Development of friendships

Literary Objectives
1. Analyze character development, symbols and theme
2. Identify and analyze the point of view
3. Identify the characteristics of a mystery
4. Identify use of simile and metaphor

Companion Titles
1. *Bridge to Terabithia* - Katherine Paterson (development of friendships, coping with unique talents and gifts, family conflicts, dealing with death)
2. *Jacob Have I Loved* - Katherine Paterson (family conflicts, coping with unique talents and gifts, development of friendships)
3. *Otherwise Known as Sheila the Great* - Judy Blume (family conflict, development of friendships, growing up)

From the Mixed-up Files of Mrs. Basil E. Frankweiler
Letter and Chapters 1–3

Vocabulary

injustice   fatigue   extravagant   knapsacks   fussbudget
Neanderthal

1. If you were fed up and bored, where would you want to spend two weeks? How would you manage? How would you eat, sleep, bathe?

2. Why did Claudia run away? Was that a good idea? Why or why not?

3. What is injustice and how did it fit into her decision?

4. Would it be boring to be "straight-A's Claudia Kincaid?" How would you feel about it?

5. Why was Jamie a good companion? Describe his characteristics that appealed to Claudia.

6. When have you used flattery to manipulate someone? How does flattery apply to this story?

7. Give a short description of Claudia's family and its members.

8. "Asides" are information for the reader or audience that the characters do not have. In this section of the book, what did the asides tell you? Are they necessary?

9. Explain what a team really means. How did Jamie and Claudia become a team?

10. What kind of traits did Claudia possess that helped to make her plan work?

11. How might Claudia have done financially if Jamie were not with her? How did you conclude this?

From the Mixed-up Files of Mrs. Basil E. Frankweiler
Chapters 4-5

Vocabulary

sarcophagus   embalm   acquisitions   curators   Michelangelo
mediocre   amassed   conclusive   humility

1. Jamie and Claudia thought that their stomachs felt like tubes of toothpaste that had been all squeezed out. Make a new simile to describe the discomfort.

2. What was the purpose of manning their stations?

3. Explain the opportunity that Jamie and Claudia had that few other children had and how they should take advantage of it.

4. Describe some useful, informative things you have learned when you were not in a classroom in school. Rank five of your skills in order of importance.

5. What is one other way the Kincaid children could have obtained a newspaper without stealing it? How do you feel about what they did?

6. What was special about the statue?

7. Who was Mrs. Basil E. Frankweiler and what was her involvement in the story?

8. Claudia and Jamie wanted to find out whether or not Michelangelo was the sculptor of Angel. Were they approaching the task correctly? How would you go about finding out?

9. Explain the passage, "I keep telling you that often the search proves more profitable than the goal." Do you agree? Why or why not?

10. Claudia and Jamie had a new source of income. What was it?

11. How were Jamie and Claudia typical brother and sister?

From the Mixed-up Files of Mrs. Basil E. Frankweiler
Chapters 6-8

Vocabulary

diagram   shepherded   solemnly   quarried

1. What daily jobs or routines were important to Claudia and why?

2. What are some ways you could describe how Sunday feels? Write several similes to describe it. Identify which of these are how Claudia and Jamie's Sunday would feel.

3. Why would Claudia risk her safety to see the Angel?

4. What did Claudia intend to accomplish before going home? Why did she feel this accomplishment was necessary?

5. The letter from the Public Relations Department stated that there were three possibilities about Angel. What were they?

6. At the end of Chapter 8, Claudia had a hunch. What is a hunch? What was hers about?

7. In Chapter 8, Jamie alluded to the quote, "You can't have your cake and eat it too." Explain this.

8. Explain how the children got the first clue about Angel and what they did with this information?

9. What portion of the museum did the children like best? What would you have enjoyed the most?

10. Why do you think Claudia selected the museum as a place to hide?

From the Mixed-up Files of Mrs. Basil E. Frankweiler
Chapters 9-10

Vocabulary
ascended   Renaissance   sauntered   bribery   authenticity

1. What conclusions did the children draw about Mrs. Frankweiler's wealth? Why did they think this?

2. What was safe about having money? Explain. What did Jamie say they traded for that safety?

3. The point of view changed in Chapter 9. How? Why do you suppose the author did this?

4. Why did it seem that Mrs. Frankweiler treated the children a bit rudely?

5. The author used the metaphor, "The eyes are the window of the soul." What does this really mean?

6. Claudia made the statement that seemed ambiguous concerning the statue being cherished like a member of her own family. How was this ambiguous?

7. Did running away make Claudia different? Support your views.

8. How did finding the secret change everything else to Claudia?

9. What gifts did the children receive from Mrs. Frankweiler? How were they significant?

10. What secrets were revealed in the end? What problems are often associated with secrets?

From the Mixed-up Files of Mrs. Basil E. Frankweiler
Conclusion and Summary

1. Claudia wanted her parents to appreciate her more. Do you think her parents did appreciate her more after she and Jamie ran away? Did she appreciate her parents more after running away? Support your views.

2. The children had a perfect opportunity to learn so much in the museum. Could a person learn everything about any topic? Why or why not? What are some things you could have learned in the museum?

3. What are some reasons for people to go to museums?

4. Claudia and Jamie quickly designed a routine for their life in the museum. What are the advantages and disadvantages of a routine?

5. The author says, "Happiness is excitement that has found a settling down place." What techniques has she used in making this comparison? What does it mean?

6. A person's philosophy is his or her beliefs, system of ideas, or principles. What was Mrs. Frankweiler's philosophy of life?

7. Claudia says, "Five minutes of planning are worth fifteen minutes of looking." To what was she referring? Was she correct? Think of another phrase to express the same idea.

8. When people go on searches, they look for something important. They might look for an important lost article, their identity, or a friend. What have you searched for in your life? Were you successful? How does your search compare to Claudia's?

9. Make a list of ways that Claudia and Jamie are different and another list of ways they are alike.

10. What did Claudia learn about herself during this story?

From the Mixed-up Files of Mrs. Basil E. Frankweiler
Activities

1. Claudia says, "We just traded safety for adventure." Think of three examples in history where people traded safety for adventure. Was it a good idea? Why? Write a short essay to explain.

2. List three to five things that you are not satisfied with in your life and explain how you can improve these things.

3. Design an advertisement to increase museum attendance during times of low attendance.

4. Create with clay your version of the angel and write a short description.

5. Research Michelangelo and give an oral report to the class.

6. Write an epilogue that includes the children meeting their parents and relating their tale of the museum.

7. Visit a museum and report to your class the details of several exhibits.

8. Read another book by Elaine Konigsburg and compare the characters of the two books.

9. Think of another title for this book and design a new cover for the book.

10. Write to the Metropolitan Museum of Art to obtain more information about the museum and their collections and exhibits. Compare the kind of exhibits you could expect to see at the Metropolitan to another art museum you have visited.

My Side of the Mountain
Jean George

Suggested Reading Level
Grades 4-5

Biography
Jean George was born in 1919 in Washington, D.C. She served as a reporter for a news service in Washington for a time. George also worked as a reporter-artist. She illustrated many of her own works. A great number of her books deal with the natural sciences as evidenced in *My Side of the Mountain*. This book was awarded the Newbery runner-up award in 1960 and was filmed by Paramount in 1969. Other works include *Dipper of Copper Creek*, *Who Really Killed Cock Robin?* and *Julie of the Wolves*. She co-authored several books with her husband John George.

Synopsis
Realistic Fiction
Sam Gribley is determined to return to his great grandfather's farm in the Catskill Mountains. He is eager to learn about survival in the wilderness. After running away to the mountains, he meets many unique characters with whom he develops very special friendships. He runs away to fulfill a dream and in the end his family joins him on the old farm. This is a very heart-warming story.

Themes
1. Survival in the wilderness
2. Family conflict
3. Human interaction with nature
4. Development of friendships
5. Developing independence

Literary Objectives
1. Identify and analyze the point of view
2. Identify and analyze character development
3. Evaluate character's actions
4. Identify the use of simile and personification

Companion Titles
1. *The Sign of the Beaver* - Elizabeth Speare (survival in the wilderness, human interaction with nature)
2. *Island of the Blue Dolphins* - Scott O'Dell (survival in the wilderness, human interaction with nature)
3. *From the Mixed-Up Files of Mrs. Basil E. Frankweiler* - E.L. Konisgburg (family conflict, developing independence)
4. *The Cay* - Theodore Taylor (survival, interdependence, interaction with nature)

My Side of the Mountain
I Hole Up in a Snowstorm – I Find Many Useful Plants

Vocabulary

hemlock   Catskill   tethers   gorge   tinder   whittle
grub   boughs   migration   mussels   loam

1. Describe Sam's tree home. How was Sam like a squirrel in his new home?

2. Describe Sam's friends of the forest in the first few chapters.

3. What is the background of the Gribley Farm?

4. What preparations had Sam made for his trip to the mountain? How did he know what he might need?

5. Sam told several people of his intention to run away and survive on the land. How did each of them react to his news?

6. How did Bill help Sam learn a valuable lesson? How might Sam use that information?

7. What impact did Miss Turner have on Sam's life?

8. Why were trees important to Sam?

My Side of the Mountain
The Old, Old Tree – The First Man Who Was After Me

Vocabulary

flanges   coltish   botanical   talons   acrid

1. Why did Sam need a house that would not be easily seen?

2. Sam boiled water without pans. How did he accomplish this?

3. How did Sam use fire to his advantage?

4. How did the story's point of view involve the reader?

5. In what ways did the little old lady's arrival on the mountain affect Sam?

6. A simile is the comparison of two things using the words "like" or "as." The author used a simile to describe the old lady's hold on Sam. Write it down and create two others that give a similar meaning.

7. Why would a falcon be useful to Sam? Describe its useful characteristics. Rank these in order of importance to Sam.

8. Why did Sam want to avoid the forest uniform?

My Side of the Mountain
I Learn to Season My Food – I Find a Real Live Man

Vocabulary
residue   harassing   niche   poaching   hysterics
vengeance   venison

1. How did Sam obtain his first deer after all?

2. How had the Baron taken on human characteristics from Sam's point of view?

3. Describe the process for making deerskin usable.

4. What changes did summer bring to Sam? How did he adapt?

5. Why did Bando come to the mountain?

6. Why did Bando select the name Thoreau for Sam?

7. Why did Bando think his life was dull compared to Sam's on the mountain?

8. What skills or ideas did Bando share with Sam?

9. After Bando left, how did Sam readjust to life without a human companion?

My Side of the Mountain
The Autumn Provides – Trouble Begins

Vocabulary

mantle   ventilate   scheme   ferocity   indignity
cavort   venison

1. The opening paragraph is an example of personification. The author stated, "September blazed a trail into the mountains." When an author uses personification, he/she gives a human characteristic to something that is not human. Find another example in Chapter 13 and explain its meaning.

2. What evidence was there to let Sam know the season was changing?

3. Why did loneliness bother Sam at this point in the story?

4. How did Frightful save Sam's life? Could a human have been more helpful? Explain.

5. How did Sam celebrate Halloween?

6. Find an example of a simile from the Halloween story.

7. Who were some of Sam's guests at the Halloween party?

8. How did the animals make Sam feel as if he had human company?

9. What were Sam's problems involving hunting season?

10. How was one man's misfortune an advantage for Sam?

11. List several skills that Sam now had. How could he use three of these in his adult life?

My Side of the Mountain
I Pile Up Wood – I Learn About Birds and People

Vocabulary

plumage   conspicuous   portico   cache   sensationalism
sanguine

1. Some people might complain of boredom or loneliness if they were in Sam's situation. How did Sam prevent or avoid boredom?

2. What evidence was there to support the idea that Sam was a careful planner? Give two or three examples.

3. How did the false reports of Sam get to the newspapers?

4. Sam realized that Bando was pleased to spend Christmas with him. What clues were given?

5. What questions or thoughts might have gone through Sam's mind when his father arrived on the mountain?

6. How did Mr. Gribley compliment his son?

7. Describe Sam and Bando's relationship. How was it different from Sam and his father's relationship? How was it similar?

8. What was Mr. Gribley's purpose in coming to the mountain?

9. What conditions might have forced Mr. Gribley into taking Sam back home with him?

My Side of the Mountain
I Have a Good Look – The City Comes to Me

Vocabulary

avalanched   barometer   concoction   resilient   conceded
forums

1. How did Sam's health affect his life in the Catskills?

2. Describe Sam's problem during the ice storm. What was different about the forest after it was over?

3. Toward the end of January, Sam had some problems with his body. What were they and how did he take care of the problems?

4. Frightful was different from others of her kind. How was she different? Why was she different?

5. What was Sam's motive in telling Matt about the wild boy?

6. What tipped Matt off to the truth about the wild boy?

7. Explain what Matt meant about "private voices." Give a personal example.

8. When Bando and Matt were both visiting Sam, something occurred to Sam about his life in the wilderness at this point. What was that thought? How was it different than what it seemed?

9. How did Sam feel about the reunion with his family?

My Side of the Mountain
Conclusion and Summary

1. Explain the reason for Sam running away from home. Was it a good reason? Why or why not? Did Sam accomplish his goal for leaving?

2. Give examples of Sam using natural resources. How did he use them efficiently?

3. Tell why it was important to Sam to set up his house on his great-grandfather's farm.

4. List three of Sam's friends and tell how each helped him in some way.

5. What was one of Sam's biggest fears? Why? How did he overcome it?

6. Describe Sam's clothing and how it was made.

7. Give an example of Sam's appreciation for nature and the animals.

8. Why was Sam's journal so important to him?

9. Was the ending a good ending for the book? Why or why not?

10. Several people influenced Sam's life. Describe who they were and how they influenced Sam. Choose three people who have had the greatest influence on **your** life and write a paragraph about each one and his or her influence.

My Side of the Mountain
Activities

1. Make a map of the Catskill Mountain area. Label and color.

2. Watch the movie version of *My Side of the Mountain*. Compare and contrast it with the book. List three scenes that were better in the book and three that were better in the movie.

3. Obtain a Boy or Girl Scout manual. Select two activities similar to the tasks Sam accomplished in the woods. Demonstrate for the class.

4. Research falcons. Prepare a speech with a visual aid to share your information about the birds.

5. Make a leaf collection or illustrations of leaves from trees mentioned in the book. Give a brief description of each type of tree mentioned.

6. Research Henry David Thoreau. Write a paper describing his life and contributions. Explain why Bando referred to Sam as Thoreau.

7. Prepare a glossary of terms relating to nature. You may illustrate where possible.

8. Read another Jean George book and compare the two books, focusing on the nature aspects of the books.

9. Make a list of items you would put in a survival kit that would help you survive in the woods. Explain how you would use each item.

10. Research plants that are native to your area. Find out which ones are edible and which ones are not. Make a display of information and plant samples.